THE NATIVE AMERICANS

INDIANS OF THE GREAT PLAINS

TRADITIONS, HISTORY, LEGENDS, AND LIFE

THE NATIVE AMERICANS

INDIANS OF THE GREAT PLAINS

TRADITIONS, HISTORY, LEGENDS, AND LIFE

LISA SITA

COURAGE BOOKS

AN IMPRINT OF RUNNING PRESS
PHILADELPHIA • LONDON

Published in the United States in 1997
by Courage Books, an imprint of
Running Press Book Publishers.

Printed in the United Kingdom by Butler & Tanner Limited

9 8 7 6 5 4 3 2 1

Digit on the right indicates the number of this printing

ISBN 0-7624-0073-0

Library of Congress Cataloging-in-Publication Number 96-69254

THE NATIVE AMERICANS
INDIANS OF THE GREAT PLAINS
was prepared and produced by
Michael Friedman Publishing Group, Inc.
15 West 26th Street
New York, New York 10010

Editor: Tony Burgess
Art Director: Lynne Yeamans
Layout: Robbi Oppermann Firestone
Photography Editors: Colleen A. Branigan and Kathryn Culley

Color separations by Ocean Graphic International Company Ltd.

Published by Courage Books,
an imprint of Running Press Book Publishers
125 South Twenty-second Street
Philadelphia, Pennsylvania 19103-4399

Contents

INTRODUCTION

The First Americans

North America was home to many diverse and interesting cultures long before Europeans arrived on American shores. Although archaeologists are not sure exactly how long the continent has been inhabited, most agree that humans have been in North America for more than eleven thousand years. Over the course of thousands of years, the first Americans gradually traveled and settled throughout the Americas, adapting to the climate and terrain of the regions in which they lived. They developed communities rich in spiritual and artistic traditions.

The traditional lifestyles of Native peoples living on the Great Plains continued uninterrupted until relatively late in history, because the Plains was one of the last places in North America to be settled by Europeans. Established trade routes, however, brought European goods to the Plains well before the Europeans themselves arrived in the region. Hence, by the time some Plains groups made their first contact with Europeans, they were already using such items as glass beads, metal knives, and horses to further improve their rich cultures.

In this book, we will explore Plains cultures as they existed before contact with European people. Because these precontact groups did not keep written

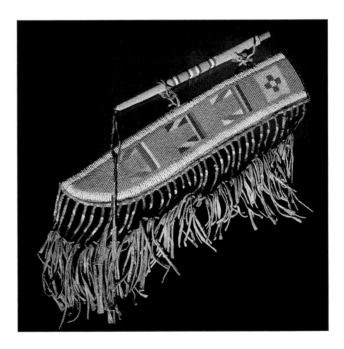

✺ THE PLAINS PEOPLES USED GLASS BEADS, A EUROPEAN TRADE ITEM, TO DECORATE ITEMS SUCH AS THIS KNIFE SHEATH AND AWL CASE.

records, we must turn to other sources in order to learn about their ways of life. Much of what we know comes from artifacts, such as tools made of stone and bone, discovered by archaeologists. Two other important sources are the information provided by Plains peoples today about the customs of their ancestors and the written accounts of the earliest European

PLAINS PEOPLES MADE AND USED RITUAL PIPES FOR CENTURIES. MANY CONTINUE THIS PRACTICE TODAY.

explorers and traders. Together these sources help researchers better understand the traditional life of Plains peoples.

CHAPTER ONE

The Great Plains

🌾 A Wide and Open Land

It is important to learn about the terrain and climate of the region before examining Plains culture, for these elements had a large impact on the peoples who lived there. The Great Plains is a vast grassland at the center of the North American continent. Stretching east to west from the Mississippi River to the Rocky Mountains, and north to south from the Saskatchewan river basin to central Texas, it is a place of swaying grasses, steadily blowing winds, and extreme weather changes. In winter, snow covers the ground, and the temperature frequently drops to -4 degrees Fahrenheit (-20 degrees Celsius). In summer, the temperature can easily rise to almost 90 degrees Fahrenheit (32 degrees Celsius). Flash downpours of cold rain are common in the summer, sometimes lasting only a few minutes before the sky clears.

The Plains is a land of few trees with rivers and streams cutting through it. Much of the landscape consists of rolling hills of grass, though some areas are relatively level, scattered with groves or single trees. In some areas, the hills are high and heavily wooded. Still other areas are dry, eroded lands called "badlands."

The western portion of the Plains receives less rain than the eastern portion. As winds blow from the west coast of North America, they carry moisture from the Pacific Ocean. This moisture falls in the form of rain and snow over the Rocky Mountains so that by the time the winds pass the Rockies and blow onto the western plains, the air is much drier. The scant rainfall, about

🌾 THE GREAT PLAINS, WHICH FORMS THE CENTRAL PART OF THE UNITED STATES, IS AN AREA OF OPEN, GRASSY LAND.

ten to twenty inches (25 to 50cm) per year, causes the grasses in the western plains to be relatively short. As the winds continue across the Great Plains, they pick up new moisture coming down from Canada and up from the Gulf of Mexico. By the time the winds reach the eastern plains, they drop enough moisture (twenty to forty inches [50 to 100cm] of rain per year) to cause the grasses to grow extremely tall, sometimes more than five feet (1½ m) high. Because of this growth, the eastern portion of the Great Plains is called the Tall Grass Plains, or the Prairie. The western area, where the grasses can be anywhere from under two feet to about four feet (60 to 122cm) tall, is called the Short Grass Plains, or the High Plains.

Because of the Plains' tough weather conditions, only hardy plants are able to thrive there. Grasses such as buffalo grass and gamma grass fare well, as do other sturdy plants including yucca, cactus, and sagebrush. Cottonwood and willow trees grow in groves in the valleys, while juniper and pine trees grow on hills and along ridges in canyons. The Plains is also home to a variety of animals, including bison (commonly called buffalo), pronghorn antelope, mule deer, coyotes, prairie chickens, grouse, elk, mountain goats, bighorn sheep, wolves, bears, eagles, and meadowlarks.

Peoples of the Plains

Two different kinds of lifestyles developed on the Great Plains. In the east, where rainfall was more plentiful and where there was access to major rivers, people lived in villages for most of the year and farmed crops such as corn, beans, and squash. The farming peoples also gathered wild plant foods, hunted wild game close to their villages, and ventured farther away for bison hunting expeditions after the spring planting and autumn harvest. Among such groups were the Omaha, Osage, Mandan, Pawnee, and Ponca.

WILDLIFE OF THE PLAINS

The following are only a few of the various types of plants and animals found on the Great Plains.

Mammals

Bison

Coyote

Red Fox

Wolf

Black-tailed Jackrabbit

Pronghorn Antelope

Prairie Dog

Mule Deer

LEFT: COYOTE CUB

ABOVE: RED FOX

Birds and Reptiles

Grouse

Red-tailed Hawk

Eagle

Lizard

Vulture

Rattlesnake

ABOVE: SAGE GROUSE

LEFT: TURKEY VULTURES

Trees and Other Plants

Sagebrush

Cottonwood

Gamma Grass

Yucca Cactus

Sunflower

Mesquite

ABOVE: SUNFLOWER

ABOVE: SAGEBRUSH

ABOVE: BISON

BELOW: MULE DEER

ABOVE: BLACK-TAILED JACKRABBIT

RIGHT: PRAIRIE RATTLESNAKE

LEFT: COLLARED LIZARD

LEFT: MESQUITE TREE

LEFT: COTTONWOOD TREE

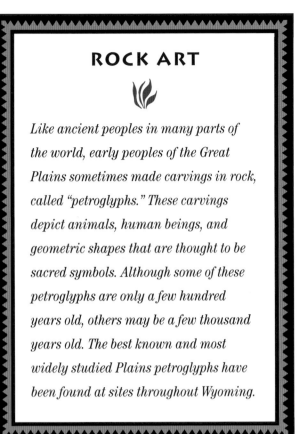
Other groups, principally those living in the western part of the Plains, where rainfall was scarce, did not farm. Instead, these peoples, such as the Blackfeet, Arapaho, Assiniboine, Crow, and Comanche, lived a nomadic lifestyle based on hunting animals and gathering wild plants. Especially important was the hunting of bison, which provided much of what the people needed, including food, blankets, and cooking utensils (see p. 30).

Years ago, many researchers thought the Great Plains was uninhabited by humans before Europeans arrived on the continent. These researchers reasoned that Native peoples could venture onto the Plains only after horses and guns had been introduced through trade. It was not possible, they argued, that people could survive in such an environment, where crops would not grow in most areas and where an important natural resource was a huge and dangerous animal. But these early theorists were misguided. Archaeological evidence shows that for more than eleven thousand years, human beings have populated the Great Plains, using their knowledge of the environment to adapt to its challenges.

One of the most important and exciting archaeological finds in North America occurred in 1926

CLAY POTS MADE BY THE HIDATSA AND MANDAN PEOPLES

humans have been in the Western Hemisphere for about eleven thousand years, others place humans there as early as forty thousand years ago or more.)

Since the Folsom discovery, archaeologists excavating the Great Plains region have uncovered evidence of mammoth hunts as well as chipped and ground stone tools that were used for cutting and scraping, and awls and ornaments made of bone and antler. These discoveries show that the Great Plains (even the drier western

⚜ THIS HISTORICAL PHOTOGRAPH SHOWS A CROW COUPLE WEARING TRADITIONAL-STYLE CLOTHING. THE WOMAN'S DRESS, MADE OF TRADE CLOTH, IS DECORATED WITH ELK TEETH.

in Folsom, New Mexico. When archaeologists uncovered the remains of some ancient bison, they found amid the bones a chipped stone projectile point (a point that is usually attached to a shaft in order to make an arrow or a spear) that had belonged to an early hunter. This discovery proved for the first time that human beings were present in the New World at least ten thousand years ago. (No one knows for sure when people first inhabited the Americas. While some archaeologists estimate that

MUMMY CAVE, WYOMING

⚜

Mummy Cave, Wyoming, near Yellowstone National Park, is a site that has revealed important information about early human life on the Great Plains. Among the many finds made by archaeologists are beautifully crafted projectile points and bone sewing awls (pointed instruments used to punch holes in hides so that the hides could be sewn together). Archaeologists also found moccasins made of bighorn sheepskin that date to about A.D. 1300, the oldest of this type ever found.

The finds at Mummy Cave cover a time span of almost five thousand years, during which the cave was used as a shelter. The cave was named for a mummy found there, the remains of a man who had died about A.D. 1300 and whose body was naturally preserved.

🌿 In this painting of a prehistoric mastodon, artist Charles R. Knight depicts what North America probably looked like during the Ice Ages.

area) has been inhabited for more than eleven thousand years. Archaeologists refer to the Native Americans of this early time period as "Paleo-Indians."

This early period of prehistory, during which the earth experienced several Ice Ages, is called the "Pleistocene." For the Paleo-Indians living during the latter part of the Pleistocene, it was a time of big-game hunting, when the main sources of food and hides in North

THE GREAT PLAINS

For thousands of years, the Plains peoples moved from one location to another. The nomadic groups ranged about as hunters and gatherers following the bison herds, and the farming peoples moved their village sites whenever drought or overuse of soil made farming difficult in their region.

During what is known as the "Historical period" (beginning in the sixteenth century), the Great Plains was inhabited by many groups of peoples who had migrated from surrounding areas. Two important factors underlying these migrations were the horse and the gun. Horses made travel easier, and thus some groups chose to move farther onto the Plains and follow the lifestyle of the nomadic bison hunter.

The gun, on the other hand, played a part in forcing some groups to move. Native peoples in the Northeast Woodlands were among the first to encounter Europeans and obtain firearms through trade. With this devastating new advantage in warfare, these groups were able to push other peoples living on the eastern fringes of the Plains without guns farther west.

This map shows the location of the Plains peoples during the mid-1800s.

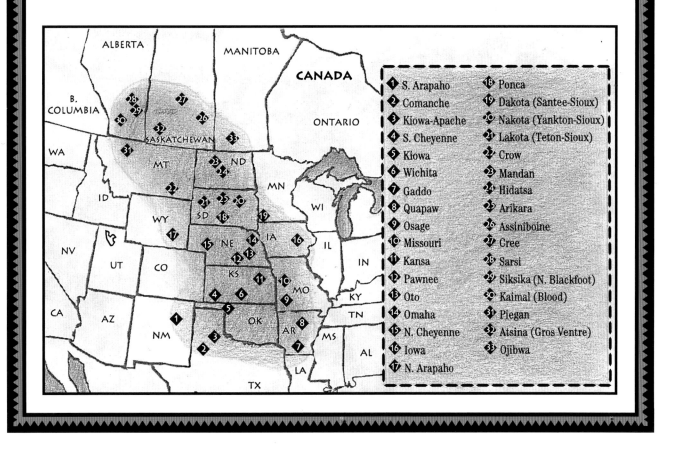

1. S. Arapaho
2. Comanche
3. Kiowa-Apache
4. S. Cheyenne
5. Kiowa
6. Wichita
7. Gaddo
8. Quapaw
9. Osage
10. Missouri
11. Kansa
12. Pawnee
13. Oto
14. Omaha
15. N. Cheyenne
16. Iowa
17. N. Arapaho
18. Ponca
19. Dakota (Santee-Sioux)
20. Nakota (Yankton-Sioux)
21. Lakota (Teton-Sioux)
22. Crow
23. Mandan
24. Hidatsa
25. Arikara
26. Assiniboine
27. Cree
28. Sarsi
29. Siksika (N. Blackfoot)
30. Kaimal (Blood)
31. Piegan
32. Atsina (Gros Ventre)
33. Ojibwa

ARENA AND CRAFTS OF THE PLAINS

ARTS AND CRAFTS OF THE PLAINS

Plains cultures were well known for their clothes and horse trappings made of bison skins and decorated with porcupine quill embroidery and, later, with beaded designs. The first beads used were blue, black, and white pony beads, with which women created bold designs in black and white or blue and white. After 1830, seed beads, which were smaller and came in more colors, became popular. By 1870, translucent beads were available. These beads were smaller than pony beads but larger than seed beads and came in even richer colors and a variety of shapes. Beaded garments were quite heavy: a beaded shirt could weigh four pounds (2kg).

Each Plains culture used distinct designs and techniques, traditions that continue among today's beadworkers. In the Southern Plains, the Kiowa and Comanche favored light, delicate bead trim. Kiowa designs also have a beaded abstract floral element made using an overlay stitch technique and the gourd or peyote stitch, which is actually a form of bead netting. It is believed that the Kiowa learned both techniques when the Delaware peoples from the East Coast moved to the Texas area in 1829. In contrast to the Kiowa, the Sioux of North and South Dakota covered large areas of clothing with beads. Sioux, Cheyenne, and Arapaho designs tend to be geometric.

Most groups also painted rawhide articles such as parfleche containers, shields, tipis, tipi linings, and robes.

In addition, the Plains peoples are known for their stone and wood carving, including elaborate stone pipes and beautiful wooden flutes.

Feather work was another important craft. Plains peoples were famed for their flowing feather war bonnets. They also used feathers to decorate shields, pipe stems, coup sticks, banners, shirts, and leggings.

America were large animals such as the mammoth, mastodon, and giant bison. By about 8000 B.C., the Pleistocene had come to an end, and climates across the globe were becoming warmer and drier.

Although the warming trend occurred worldwide, significant changes in climate occurred in different parts of the world at different times. On the Great Plains, this change began about 5000 B.C., ushering in a period known as the Archaic. By this time, the large Ice Age mammals had become extinct. During this time, some peoples migrated out of the area, but those who remained on the Great Plains adapted to the new environment by gathering wild plants and berries and by hunting and trapping smaller game.

The Archaic lifestyle dominated the Great Plains until about 250 B.C. Meanwhile, in the eastern plains, new traditions arose that eventually led to a period known as the Plains Woodland, which lasted from about 500 B.C. to about A.D. 950, though some Archaic traditions survived well into this period. During the Plains

Woodland period, eastern Plains groups began to live in semipermanent villages, build burial mounds for their dead, make pottery, and farm in a limited way. Over time, farming developed and eventually became a standard practice in addition to hunting. This period of new development, called the "Plains Village," followed the Plains Woodland and lasted well into the period of European contact. Although influences of the farming peoples reached farther west during the Plains Woodland and Plains Village periods, small groups of nomadic peoples continued to follow a strictly hunting and gathering way of life on the western plains.

In general, the Plains peoples were expert hunters who devised clever techniques for killing bison. These peoples developed complex spiritual traditions based on the sacredness of all living things and underwent difficult rituals to better understand their spiritual teachings and become closer to the Creator and the spirit world. Using only the natural resources at hand, they crafted beautiful objects for everyday use and designed one of the most effective portable homes ever invented. These achievements, and others, came before contact with outsiders on the Great Plains.

🌾 THE FRONT (TOP) AND BACK (BOTTOM) VIEWS OF A CEREMONIAL DRUM. DRUM HEADS WERE OFTEN PAINTED WITH DESIGNS REPRESENTING SPIRITS AND IMAGES FROM THEIR OWNERS' VISIONS.

CHAPTER TWO

The Bison

The Hunt

The most important animal hunted by all Plains peoples was the bison. Before European contact and the introduction of the horse, hunting was done on foot. Plains peoples hunted bison in various ways, relying on their understanding of the animal's behavior for a successful hunt.

One hunting method was to sneak up on an animal and shoot it, using a bow and arrow. Sometimes, in order to approach the bison, the hunter would cover himself with a wolf's skin. Thus, he not only looked like a wolf, but he smelled like a wolf as well. Bison in a herd are not frightened by a single wolf. Although a pack of wolves would pose a threat, a single wolf would not be able to do much harm against an entire herd of bison. Plains hunters understood this situation and used it to their advantage.

In winter, some hunters hunted on snow-shoes, which allowed them to move relatively easily on the surface of the snow. The animals, however, would get stuck. As the bison struggled to move through the snow, the hunters could easily kill them.

LEFT: HUNTERS, WEARING WOLF SKINS TO FOOL THE BISON, SNEAK UP ON THEIR PREY IN THIS PAINTING BY KARL BODMER. **ABOVE:** A BOW AND SOME ARROWS, EFFECTIVE HUNTING WEAPONS, WERE CARRIED IN A "QUIVER," OR CASE, AS SHOWN HERE.

EVIDENCE OF THE HUNT

Much of what archaeologists know about early bison hunts comes from sites where the hunts actually took place. At Olsen-Chubbuck in Colorado, for instance, archaeologists uncovered the remains of a bison drive that took place about 6500 B.C. From examining these remains, they were able to determine that the skins had been removed from the bison after they had been killed. To remove the skin of a bison, the tailbone of the animal must also be removed—the animals of Olsen-Chubbuck had had their tails detached. Skinning tools (tools used to remove the skin of an animal) were also found at the site, further proof that the hides had been removed. These skins were probably used by native peoples as clothing.

Archaeologists were also able to determine how the hunters butchered the animals. They could see that the hunters removed the animals' tongues, probably to eat them. Almost two hundred bison were killed during the hunt at Olsen-Chubbuck, and archaeologists estimate that the hunters probably obtained nearly fifty-seven thousand pounds (25,878kg) of meat along with ten thousand pounds (4,540kg) of organs and fat.

🌿 THE EXCITEMENT OF THE BISON CHASE ON HORSEBACK IS CAPTURED IN THIS NINETEENTH-CENTURY PAINTING BY WESTERN ARTIST C.M. RUSSELL.

Although bison were hunted sometimes by a single hunter or by pairs, the more common method of hunting was the communal hunt undertaken by an entire group. Communal hunts could be carried out in various ways. Sometimes the hunters simply surrounded the animals and killed them. In other instances, the hunters would set fire to the grass surrounding the animals on all sides but one. As the animals fled the fire, the hunters waiting there killed them. Probably the most popular method of communal hunting was the bison drive, which involved stampeding the animals over a cliff. Hunters would usually corral the animals before driving them over the edge. This was done by building piles of rocks in two lines leading to the edge of the cliff. The hunters would build the lines of rocks closer together as they neared the cliff, so that the two lines began to look almost like a V. To cause the herd to stampede, the hunters set fires. Trying to escape the flames, the bison would run, following the lead bison. Bison herds always have a leader, and they will always follow that leader, even to their deaths.

Meanwhile, men and women, some of them miles from the edge of the cliff, screamed and waved blankets, frightening the animals so that they would begin to run into the area between the two lines of rock piles. Other men would hide behind the rock piles by the cliff's edge and, as the bison neared, would jump up from behind the rocks to scare them onward. The bison, now at the edge, could not stop in time. Pushed by the animals behind them, they tumbled forward and were usually killed by the fall. Hunters waited below with spears and bows and arrows to kill the bison that managed to survive the long drop.

◟ The Importance of the Bison

The bison supplied most of what the Plains peoples needed. Bison meat and some of the internal organs were eaten. Bison hair was braided into ropes and used as stuffing for children's dolls, balls, and other items. Horns were made into spoons by heating them and molding them into shape. Ribs tied together formed a sled for children. Bones were carved into tools, such as hide scrapers and awls. Skulls were used in ceremonies. Sinews, which are tendons from the animal's muscles, were used as thread for sewing. Stomachs suspended from a framework of sticks were used as cooking pots to make stews of bison meat and vegetables. Because a bison stomach would burn if suspended over a fire, the method of cooking involved heating rocks and putting the hot rocks into the food that had already been placed in the bison stomach. In this way, the food would eventually heat up. In areas where trees were not plentiful, bison dung was burned for fuel. Hides provided materials for making such items as moccasins, blankets, containers, shields, and tipi covers.

The hide could be made into tough rawhide or softened into pliable leather, depending on what the hide would be used for. To prepare a hide for use, a Plains woman usually began by spreading the hide on the grass and pinning it down with wooden stakes. The next step was to remove the blood, fat, and meat still clinging to the hide with a fleshing tool, an implement made of animal bone notched at one end to form scraping teeth. The hide was then left to dry. Later, the skin was

IN THIS DRAWING, A PLAINS WOMAN POUNDS STRIPS OF DRIED BISON MEAT TO MAKE PEMMICAN.

🌿 A winter scene in a Hidatsa village. The people in the center are keeping warm by wrapping themselves in their bison robes.

FACTS ABOUT THE AMERICAN BISON

1. The bison is the largest land mammal in North America.

2. An adult male bison is called a "bull"; an adult female is called a "cow"; and a young bison is called a "calf."

3. The adult bison weighs between eight hundred and two thousand pounds (363 and 908kg). (An adult bull can weigh up to two thousand pounds and can stand six and a half feet [2m] tall. An adult cow can weigh more than one thousand pounds [454kg] and is only a little shorter than a bull.)

4. Bison move an average of two miles (3km) per day to graze.

5. When necessary, bison can run thirty-five miles per hour (56kph) and keep that pace for half an hour.

6. Both male and female bison have horns. The average bison horn is two feet (60cm) long, and the span between two bison horns can be more than two feet (60cm).

7. Researchers estimate there were at least thirty million, and perhaps as many as sixty million, bison in North America in the early 1700s. In the 1800s, Europeans hunted the bison nearly to extinction. Today, there are about sixty-five thousand bison in the United States.

PARFLECHES

Plains peoples often kept their personal belongings in colorfully decorated containers made of rawhide. One type of container, called a "parfleche," was a kind of large envelope made by folding a rectangular piece of rawhide four times: the two long ends were folded lengthwise in toward the center, and then the short ends were folded over toward the center. Once the short ends had been folded, they formed flaps that were tied together with a rawhide string. The average size of a parfleche was about two feet long by one foot wide (60 by 30cm) when fully folded. Plains women usually decorated their parfleches with brightly painted designs.

Parfleches were used to hold pemmican, a nutritious food that could be stored for long periods of time and could be carried easily when traveling. It consisted of three ingredients: strips of dried meat, dried chokecherries, and fat. First, the meat and the chokecherries were pounded with a stone hammer. Then the fat was boiled and added to the meat and chokecherries, creating a dish similar to hash. Once the mixture was complete, it was packed into parfleches.

Plains people created other types of containers, too. Some were made in the shape of cylinders and were used to hold headdresses, arrows, and other long objects. Square containers were used as bags to hold items such as tools.

A PAINTED PARFLECHE

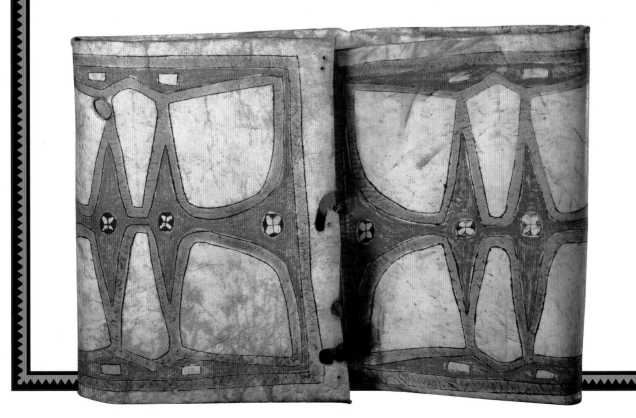

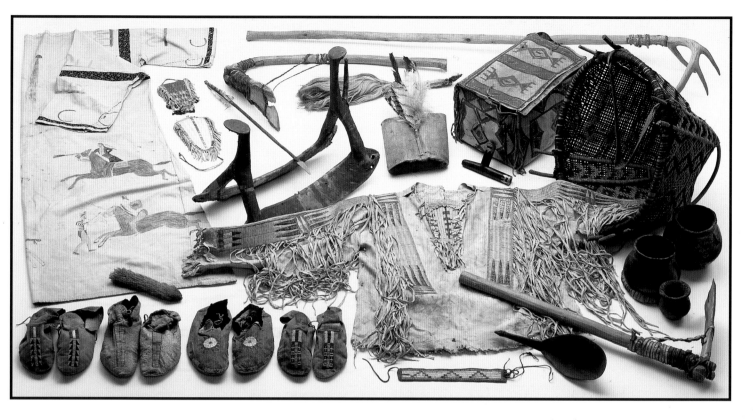

made thinner by using a scraper, an L-shaped tool usually made of bone or antler with a sharp stone or metal blade attached to it. If the woman wanted to remove the animal's hair, she would turn the hide over and scrape the hair off with the scraper. Left like this, the hide made a tough rawhide that could be used to make containers, thongs for strapping, dance rattles, and many other items.

If the hide was to be softened, the woman would continue to work on it in a number of ways. She would rub a mixture of animal brains and fat into the hide with a smooth stone, rub the hide with a bone tool, stretch the hide with her hands while holding it down with her foot, or rub it back and forth over a rawhide thong.

One important and beautiful article of clothing made from the hide of the bison was the bison robe, which helped keep the Plains peoples warm during their bitter, cold winters. A combination blanket and coat, the bison robe was a hide with the hair of the animal on one side and softened leather on the other. The robe was

ABOVE: A VARIETY OF EVERYDAY ITEMS MADE AND USED BY THE PLAINS PEOPLES, INCLUDING AN ANTLER RAKE, A BASKET FOR CARRYING HEAVY LOADS, AND A WOODEN FRAME FOR A SADDLE. **BELOW:** A CEREMONIAL RATTLE MADE OF A GOURD AND INCISED WITH THE FIGURE OF A BISON

wrapped around the body, hair side inward. The side without the hair was usually decorated with dyed porcupine quills or skillfully painted. Paints were made by crushing different colored minerals, clays, and charcoal into a powder and adding a sticky liquid that was made by boiling animal hide scrapings. The paint was applied with a piece of bone, wood, or horn. When women decorated

USES OF THE BISON

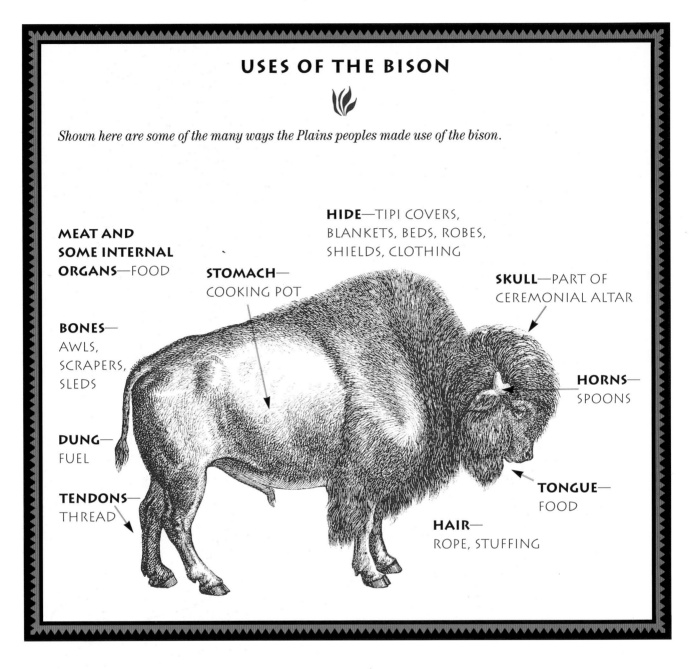

Shown here are some of the many ways the Plains peoples made use of the bison.

MEAT AND SOME INTERNAL ORGANS—FOOD

STOMACH— COOKING POT

HIDE—TIPI COVERS, BLANKETS, BEDS, ROBES, SHIELDS, CLOTHING

SKULL—PART OF CEREMONIAL ALTAR

BONES— AWLS, SCRAPERS, SLEDS

HORNS— SPOONS

DUNG— FUEL

TENDONS— THREAD

TONGUE— FOOD

HAIR— ROPE, STUFFING

robes, they usually painted geometric designs. Men painted figures of people and animals in scenes representing important events, such as wars and hunts, in which the men themselves had been involved.

Although the bison was the most important resource for the Plains peoples, it was not the only one. Other animals, such as deer and elk, were also hunted. They provided food, bones and antlers for tools, and hides for clothing. Food was also obtained by gathering various wild fruits and vegetables, such

❧ OPPOSITE: PLAINS MEN PAINTED SCENES AND FIGURES ON THEIR BISON ROBES AS A WAY OF RECORDING IMPORTANT EVENTS.

as prairie turnips, plums, and chokecherries. Among agricultural peoples, women grew corn, beans, squash, pumpkins, and sunflowers, which were often traded to groups that did not farm.

CHAPTER THREE

The Dog and the Horse

❦ The Importance of the Dog

Two domesticated animals played important roles in the Plains cultures. The first of these was the dog, which was used as a pack animal long before the introduction of the horse. (At Agate Basin in Wyoming, archaeologists have found the remains of a domesticated dog that dates back 10,800 years. Domesticated dogs can be distinguished from wild dogs because the former have larger jaws and smaller teeth that are more worn down as a result of eating scraps.) For nomadic peoples who moved frequently in search of resources, the dog was especially helpful.

When a herd of bison was located by scouts, the people packed their belongings in preparation to move. Once packed, the belongings were either strapped to a dog's back or to a travois. The travois was a device made of two poles lashed together at the top, forming an A shape, with strips of rawhide across the midsection of the A. Tipis were dismantled, and the folded covers, along with the poles, were also strapped to the travois. The upper part of the travois was then attached to the shoulders of a dog, which dragged the vehicle behind it.

The dog travois was used not only to move from one camp to another, but also to bring hides, butchered meat, and firewood back to an established campsite or village. Depending on the strength of the dog, loads

❦ A GROUP OF PLAINS PEOPLE MOVING CAMP. ALTHOUGH HORSES WERE ABLE TO DRAG HEAVIER LOADS THAN DOGS, DOGS CONTINUED TO BE KEPT AS DOMESTICATED ANIMALS AFTER HORSES WERE INTRODUCED.

A DOG WITH A TRAVOIS HARNESSED TO ITS SHOULDERS

Horses and Change

In the sixteenth, seventeenth, and eighteenth centuries, a small number of Europeans (Spanish explorers coming up from the Southwest and the Southeast and French explorers and fur traders coming down from the Northeast) came to the Great Plains. A few of the Plains groups made contact with these outsiders. However, through established trade routes, many other Plains peoples acquired European goods, including guns, ammunition, glass beads, metal knives, and horses, without actually seeing the Europeans themselves.

Of all the elements introduced by Europeans, horses—and to a large extent guns—were the most significant. With the introduction of the horse, the lifestyle of the Plains peoples changed dramatically. The animals were introduced to North America by the Spanish, who brought them first to Mexico and then to the Southwest in the sixteenth century. By the early 1700s, horses had come to the Great Plains. This happened slowly at first, through trade and by raiding, but by the late 1700s horses were common.

With horses, the Plains people were able to move around more freely and easily. Some groups living more sedentary lives east and west of the High Plains moved farther inward and adopted a nomadic life of bison hunting. Tracking bison herds on horseback was

generally ranged from thirty-five to fifty pounds (16 to 23kg), though a strong dog could drag about seventy-five pounds (34kg).

With no other animals to help them, the Plains peoples attached special significance to their dogs and enjoyed a close relationship with them. They gave their dogs names and praised their strength. Sometimes dogs accompanied men on war and hunting parties. The Blackfeet, for example, trained their dogs to scare smaller game out of hiding places. The Crow and the Cree took dogs with them on long journeys so that these animals could carry extra pairs of moccasins should the men need them. Dogs were also guardians that protected the camp or village.

PREHISTORIC HORSES IN NORTH AMERICA

Although Spanish explorers were the first people to take the modern horse to the Americas, horses did exist there millions of years ago. Called Hyracotherium vasacciense and popularly known as Eohippus, the earliest known horse roamed North America about fifty-five million years ago. At that time, North America looked very different than it does today: it was tropical, with lush vegetation. Compared to the modern horse, Eohippus was very small, about the size of a sheep. Instead of hooves it had three toes on its hind feet and four on its front. Over millions of years, as the climate of North America changed and became cooler, Eohippus evolved. The limbs lengthened, and hooves came to replace the toes on all four feet. For reasons that are still unclear, the prehistoric horse in North America became extinct by about 9000 B.C.

ARTIST CHARLES R. KNIGHT'S DEPICTION OF WHAT EOHIPPUS PROBABLY LOOKED LIKE.

easier and faster than tracking on foot. Because the horses allowed them to move faster and farther, hunters could take on larger bison herds. The exciting bison chase on horseback became the new method of hunting.

🌿 IN THIS NINETEENTH-CENTURY PAINTING BY GEORGE CATLIN, HORSEMEN ARE DEPICTED SHOWING THEIR SKILL. SOME RIDERS BECAME SO ADEPT THAT THEY WERE ABLE TO RIDE ALONG THE HORSE'S SIDE WITH ONE FOOT HOOKED OVER ITS BACK. THEY COULD THEN SHOOT ARROWS OVER THE HORSE'S NECK WHILE REMAINING PROTECTED.

Although the dog was still important, horses allowed heavier loads to be carried. Thus, nomadic peoples were able to build larger, more comfortable tipis, since the horses were strong enough to transport them when it was time to move to a new camp. With the aid of the horse travois, more meat and hides could be transported back to camp, so the camps were able to support greater numbers of people. Hence, the groups grew.

Horses also played a significant role in warfare. Prior to the horse, combat between groups was conducted on foot. Horses allowed warriors to fight from a mounted position, thereby making them more effective. Although the role of the warrior as a brave and skillful fighter was

always respected, it was not until horses were acquired that the Plains peoples were able to transform their warfare into the competitive match of skills for which it became well known. This way of fighting was a system known as "counting coup," in which a warrior brought honor to himself and his people by doing any number of courageous acts, including approaching an enemy and striking him with a staff or a hand, wounding him or taking his life, or saving a wounded friend. In this type of combat, a demonstration of bravery and daring was more important than the actual killing of an enemy.

Horses had further impact on warfare in that they were often the cause of it. Plains peoples soon came to depend on horses, and the animals became so valuable

IN THIS DEPICTION OF A PLAINS ENCAMPMENT, THE HORSES, BLANKETS, AND CLOTH CLOTHING WORN BY THE STANDING CHILD ARE ALL ITEMS INTRODUCED THROUGH CONTACT WITH EUROPEANS.

that sometimes raiding parties would go out for the sole purpose of taking horses from a rival camp.

Finally, horses allowed some people to enjoy prestige. A man was admired for his ability to raid for horses. Furthermore, an individual with many horses was in a better position to help others when the time came to move camp or go on a hunt. Since generosity was respected and admired, those who shared their horses were seen as notable members of the group.

CHAPTER FOUR

The Community

🕯 Growing Up

The first thing a newborn Plains baby felt against his or her skin was a blanket made from the softened skin of a bison calf. As the child grew older, he or she would learn the important role this animal played in the survival of the people. Boys would look forward to the time when they would be old enough to hunt alongside their fathers on the great bison chase. They would play at hunting, as well as at warfare, using toy bows and weapons made for them by their fathers. Girls would play with dolls stuffed with bison hair, and they would help their mothers in the preparation of hides and food. In winter, children would enjoy sliding along the snow on sleds of bison ribs lashed together with strips of tough bison rawhide.

Winter was also the time for storytelling. When the weather caused activity to slow down, children and adults alike would settle down beside the fire in their homes to hear stories. Many of the stories had morals that taught the children how to behave and what kinds of virtues to seek. Generosity, inner strength, and wisdom were among the values that were especially important in the lives of Plains peoples. Boys were encouraged to be courageous warriors and skilled

🕯 **LEFT:** TCHUNG-KEE, PLAYED WITH A HOOP AND POLE, WAS A POPULAR GAME AMONG THE MANDAN. ALMOST ALL PLAINS PEOPLE PLAYED SOME FORM OF HOOP AND POLE. **ABOVE:** PLAINS BABIES WERE USUALLY CARRIED IN A DECORATED BABY CARRIER LIKE THIS ONE.

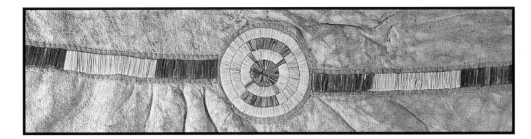

hunters, and girls were encouraged to be hardworking and skilled in traditional crafts.

One such craft was quillworking, the art of decorating clothing and other objects with porcupine quills. The quills were cleaned, dyed using dyes made from plants, and then affixed to the object to be ornamented. Although Plains women later adopted beads as a form of decoration when they became available through European trade, the art of porcupine quillwork was not totally abandoned.

THESE PLAINS WOMEN ARE PREPARING A BISON HIDE IN THE TRADITIONAL WAY USED BY THEIR ANCESTORS.

Children, as well as adults, played many kinds of games, some of which tested and developed the players' physical skills. One popular team game was the sport of Hoop and Pole. It was played by rolling a hoop along the ground and trying to stop its movement by throwing a pole through it. A hoop was usually made of flexible wood, sometimes with a netting of rawhide string stretched across its middle. Poles, too, were usually made of wood.

Another favorite game was dice. A variety of materials, including wood, bone, animal teeth, and fruit pits, were made into dice by painting or carving designs on them. Each design had a different value in the game. A player placed the dice in a basket, threw them upward,

THE CALUMET

Some Plains peoples, such as the Pawnee, Omaha, and Ponca, often used an object called a "calumet" when performing adoptions and cementing other relationships. The calumet was a hollow reed with a fan of eagle feathers attached to it.

In a special ceremony, a man could give a calumet to another person, who would become his son. At other times, one group would present a calumet or a set of calumets to another group in order to form an alliance. By "adopting" another group of people in this way, groups were able to form strong bonds and have good relations with one another.

🌿 A CALUMET OF THE CROW PEOPLE. BESIDES FEATHERS, CALUMETS WERE OFTEN EMBELLISHED WITH THE DRIED SKINS OF SMALL ANIMALS SUCH AS BIRDS AND ERMINE.

🌿 A PAIR OF MOCCASINS WITH BEADED DESIGNS. TYPICAL OF PLAINS DECORATIVE STYLE, THE PATTERNS SHOW GEOMETRIC SHAPES, INCLUDING THE CIRCLE, WHICH IS A SYMBOL OF UNITY AND THE CYCLES OF NATURE.

THE FIRST FLUTE: A LAKOTA STORY

The flutes used by young Plains men when they wanted to attract young women were usually made of cedar and shaped like the head of a bird with a long, open beak. As the man played, the flute's sound came from the bird's beak. One story from the Lakota tells how this flute came to be invented.

Long ago, a young man was out by himself hunting elk. He wandered far from home and settled for the night beneath a cedar tree. Among the many sounds of the forest, he heard a low, sad sound; but it was also a beautiful sound, a song of love and longing. When he awoke the next morning, the hunter saw a woodpecker in the branches above his head, pecking at a dead limb. Then a wind passed by, and the hunter heard the same sad, beautiful sound he had heard the night before. He looked more closely, and saw that the woodpecker had made holes in the branch, and he realized that the song came from the wind whistling through those holes.

The hunter took the branch home but could not figure out how to use the branch to make the sounds the wind had made. He went on a spiritual journey known as a vision quest (see page 55), praying for instruction in how to use the branch to play the lovely song. After many days the woodpecker appeared to the hunter in a vision. The bird spoke to the young man, showing him how to make a musical instrument from a branch and how to play songs on it.

At the end of this vision quest, the young man set to work carving the instrument, forming it into the shape of a bird's head. Using the skill the woodpecker had taught him, he played his first song on the new flute, then brought it back to his people, who were overjoyed to hear its beautiful sound. While playing his flute, the young man attracted a lovely young woman who could not resist the melodious sound. When they saw this, other young men began to make their own flutes and attract their own women, until the custom spread. Making and playing flutes became a favorite way for young people of the Plains to communicate with one another.

✣ A BIRD-HEADED COURTING FLUTE

and caught them. The score was determined by which design faced upward when the dice were caught by the player.

As children grew up, they continued to learn skills, values, and practical knowledge from parents and members of the extended family. Plains children were raised not only by their parents; grandparents, aunts, uncles, and other relatives all played significant roles in a child's education and discipline. Plains peoples also practiced adoption, so an orphaned child was never without a family; someone, usually a relative, would always accept responsibility for a child without parents.

 Marriage

When children reached young adulthood, it was time for marriage. Although marriages were often arranged by the children's parents, young people were allowed a large degree of choice in the matter, and they often selected their spouses on their own. Love and romance played a big role in these decisions, and a young man would often try to win over a special girl by playing songs to her on a wooden flute.

Most Plains marriages were monogamous—that is, a man would have only one wife and a woman would have only one husband. But sometimes a man would marry more than one woman. This usually only happened for reasons of necessity. For instance, if a man's wife was overburdened with household chores, he might take a second wife to help her. Or, if a woman were left alone because her first husband died, which happened often because of the dangers of hunting and warfare, she might become the second wife

A COMMON COURTING RITUAL AMONG YOUNG PLAINS PEOPLE WAS FOR THE COUPLE TO WRAP THEMSELVES IN A SINGLE ROBE.

of another man. This practice ensured that women always had someone to provide for them, and that no woman had more work than she could handle.

Social Organization

Aside from hunting, a man's main duty toward the group was to offer protection from enemies. His other responsibilities were to make his own weapons, including bows and arrows, lances, and war clubs; to make his own ceremonial objects; and, after the horse was introduced, to train his own horses. Women were responsible for gathering wild foods and preparing the foods by preserving and cooking them. Among agricultural groups, women also farmed. Plains women prepared bison hides for use by either making them into stiff, hard rawhide or softening them for use as clothing. Other female responsibilities included collecting firewood, fetching water, and taking care of the children. Among nomadic groups, women were in charge of dismantling the tipis and packing the belongings when it was time to move camp, as well as setting everything back up again at the new campsite.

TRADITIONAL PLAINS CLOTHING CONSISTED OF A SKIN DRESS FOR WOMEN AND A SHIRT, BREECHCLOUT, AND LEGGINGS FOR MEN. CLOTHING WAS EMBELLISHED WITH QUILLWORK, ELK TEETH, BEADWORK, FRINGES, AND, SOMETIMES, HAIR.

🌿 A CHILD'S DRESS ADORNED WITH ELABORATE BEADWORK

Depending on the time of year, a camp could consist of a band or a tribe. The band was made up of several groups of families that traveled and hunted together. The tribe, or "nation," as it is also called, consisted of several bands. (Among agricultural groups, a tribe or nation could consist of several villages.) During the colder months, from about late autumn to early spring, a band would settle into a winter campsite, because traveling was dangerous and difficult. The campsite would be established near water where there were enough trees to offer protection from the wind. Men hunted, but they stayed close enough to the campsite so that they could return the same day.

In spring and summer, the people were able to move camp more frequently, for travel was substantially easier and resources would most likely be plentiful wherever they went. As they traveled, they often met people of

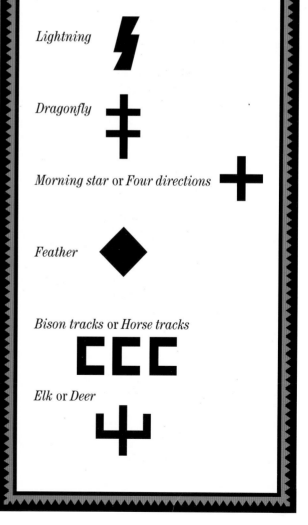

PLAINS DESIGNS

🌿

The clothing, bison robes, parfleches, and other items made by the Plains peoples were almost always beautifully and colorfully decorated. Figures of people and animals often represented real-life events or scenes from visions and dreams, while geometric designs usually had symbolic meaning. (Sometimes one design had more than one meaning.) Listed here are some of the more basic geometric designs and what they stand for.

Lightning

Dragonfly

Morning star or *Four directions*

Feather

Bison tracks or *Horse tracks*

Elk or *Deer*

other tribes who spoke languages different from their own. In order to communicate with one another, the various Plains tribes devised a system of sign language using basic gestures that everyone could understand. This system was also used when trading with the agricultural peoples.

The tribe came together in midsummer at a spot chosen during the previous year. At the designated location, the various bands formed a large camp of several hundred families near a water supply on the open plain. It was an opportunity for friends and relatives who had not seen one another all year to meet. It was also a time for the tribe to perform community rituals and make important decisions.

Decision making on the Plains was carried out under the guidance of respected leaders. Each band had its own leader, or chief, and some had several. But leaders did not control the group. They counseled and offered guidance instead of giving orders. Decisions regarding such matters as when to move camp, when to go on a hunt, or when to raid an enemy were made by all adult men of the group, based on the advice of the leaders. A man became a leader because of his merits, wisdom, and experience, so such a man was likely to be an older person who had shown bravery and generosity throughout his life and who had been a skilled warrior and hunter.

Also important in the smooth running of camp and village affairs were the various warrior societies. Each of the different societies had its own responsibilities, including acting as a kind of police force to keep order within the community, guarding the community against attacking enemies, and maintaining order during bison hunts.

PLAINS MEN IN FULL CEREMONIAL REGALIA USING SIGN LANGUAGE TO COMMUNICATE WITH ONE ANOTHER

MUSIC AND DANCE

Like Native Americans throughout North America, Plains peoples had many kinds of ceremonies that included music and dance. Singing and dancing were a form of prayer and were usually accompanied by the sound of a drum and sometimes rattles. (A third type of musical instrument was the "flageolet," or courting flute, used by a young man to attract a woman.)

Drums were made of animal hide stretched over wooden frames and were often painted with symbols and designs. The two types of drums used were the two-headed drum and the hand drum. The two-headed drum was larger than the hand drum and was suspended with hide thongs from four wooden stakes. Several individuals sat around the drum and played it at the same time using drumsticks of wood with leather tips. The

hand drum had only one head and was played by a single person who held the drum by grasping a rawhide webbing at the back.

Rattles, too, were sometimes made of rawhide. The hide was sewn into the shape of the rattle head, soaked in water, and then filled with sand. When the hide dried it became stiff. The sand was poured out, pebbles were added, and a wooden handle was attached. Rattles were also made by filling dried gourds with pebbles and attaching a handle, and by tying together parts of animal hooves and attaching them to a wooden handle so that they rattled when shaken.

IN THIS PAINTING BY GEORGE CATLIN, MANDAN WARRIORS OF THE BUFFALO BULLS SOCIETY PERFORM A CEREMONIAL DANCE.

THE WINTER COUNT

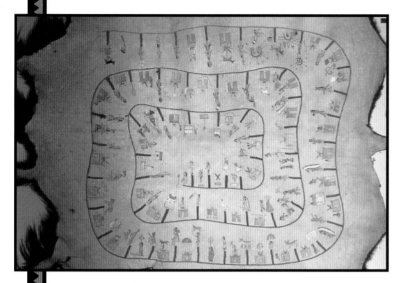

🌿 This bison-hide winter count shows the use of the spiral pattern in recording important events.

The Plains peoples, like other Native peoples of North America, traditionally did not have written languages. Instead, they relied on what is called the "oral tradition," whereby information is passed from generation to generation by remembering stories and retelling them.

To help keep track of important events, the Plains peoples kept a record called a "winter count," a piece of hide on which symbolic pictures, called "pictographs," were painted. Each pictograph represented an important event from one year in the history of the group. One person was usually in charge of keeping the winter count. This person acted as the artist, the record keeper, and the custodian of the winter count.

Each year, the people of the group would decide together what was the most significant occurrence of that year. This event could have been anything from a particularly harsh winter when there was a shortage of food to a particularly successful bison hunt. Once the event was agreed upon, the keeper of the winter count painted a pictograph of the event on the hide. On some winter counts, the pictographs were painted in straight, parallel lines, but more commonly they were painted in a circular spiral pattern, with the earliest event painted in the center of the hide.

The keeper was also responsible for remembering the details of all the events and the years in which they happened. By looking at the winter count, he could recite the people's history. To ensure that the information was passed on, the keeper had an apprentice whom he trained to be the next keeper of the winter count. When the keeper died, the apprentice would take over and become responsible for keeping the winter count. As the new keeper, he would obtain an apprentice of his own, and the entire process would repeat itself. In this way, the knowledge was passed on from generation to generation.

 # Homes

The tipi was the home of the nomadic Plains peoples, though it was also used by agricultural peoples when they left their villages to hunt bison. Because the nomadic groups traveled often, they could not be burdened with unnecessary items, and their belongings, including their homes, needed to be portable. The tipi was well suited for the environment of the western plains, for it was warm in winter and cool in summer. Moreover, it was durable enough to offer protection against the harsh winds and flash downpours of the region. The tipi could also be easily dismantled and put up again at a new campsite.

A woman made and owned her family's tipi and its furnishings. The tipi was made by tying a cover of sewn bison hides over a framework of wooden poles. These poles, lashed together at their tops by a long rawhide thong, formed a cone that sat on the surface of the ground with its point in the air. The tipi cover was attached to this framework and fastened together in the front. Two flaps at the top could be opened and closed with two additional poles. By adjusting the flaps, the people inside could allow air to enter, let smoke escape, or keep out the wind and rain. The cover was secured to the ground with wooden

A TIPI COVER WITH PAINTED SCENES. MEN PAINTED SCENES ON TIPI COVERS AND BISON ROBES AS A WAY OF RECORDING THEIR SUCCESSES IN WARFARE AND HUNTING.

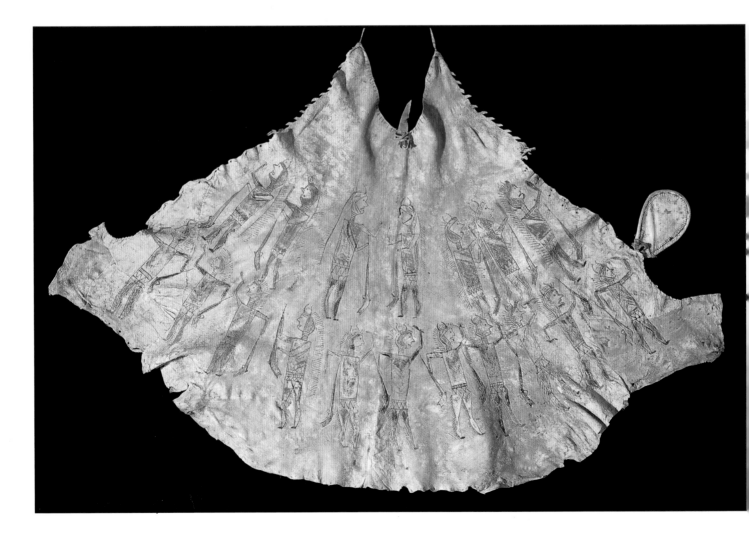

pegs, although in earlier times rocks were used instead. In warm weather, the edges could be lifted up to allow air to circulate.

Inside the tipi, a fire pit lined with rocks was dug in the center of the circle that formed the floor. Bison hides with the fur still on them were used as beds, blankets, and places to sit. Backrests were formed by hanging an A-shaped mat made of willow rods from a tripod of wooden poles. A hide lining placed along the inside of the tipi cover kept out drafts. Personal items such as shields, bows, and bags were often hung from these linings.

In pre-horse days, the tipi was usually made of six or eight bison hides and measured no more than ten feet (3m) in diameter. After the introduction of the horse, the average tipi was made of about fourteen hides and measured about fifteen feet (4½m) in diameter.

The farming peoples of the Great Plains constructed more permanent homes, since they did not move about as often as the nomadic peoples. Grass

TOP: THE TIPI WAS THE STYLE OF HOME USED YEAR-ROUND BY THE NOMADIC PEOPLES OF THE PLAINS.
ABOVE: THE WICHITA AND CADDO PEOPLES LIVED IN GRASS HOUSES.

houses, the homes of the Wichita and Caddo, consisted of a framework of wooden poles covered with grass thatch. Most farming peoples, however, lived in earthlodges, which were large, circular structures with domed roofs. An earthlodge was constructed by building a framework of heavy poles and covering it with layers of branches, grass, sod, and an outer layer of packed earth. A covered tunnel-like passageway served as the

entrance. Earthlodges were usually ten to twelve feet (3 to 3½m) high and forty-five to fifty feet (13½ to 15m) in diameter. Each dwelling could house about forty people.

Inside the home, sleeping platforms, which were usually covered with curtains made of bison skin, were built along the walls. Backrests, like those used in tipis, were also part of the furnishings. Storage pits for food were built into the ground inside as well as outside the lodge. Tools, firewood, and all personal and household items were kept within the earthlodge. Even horses, after they had been acquired from the Europeans, were kept in stalls and corrals built within the lodge.

As in the tipi, a fireplace was built in the center of the earthlodge. Smoke escaped through a hole in the roof. In bad weather, this hole could be covered by an inverted bullboat, a type of circular boat made of bison skin stretched over a wooden frame. Bullboats were used both as covers and as a means of transportation by peoples living along the upper Missouri River, including the Mandan, Hidatsa, and Arikara.

❧ IN THIS HISTORICAL PHOTOGRAPH, WOMEN OF THE UPPER MISSOURI, WEARING CLOTHING OF TRADE CLOTH, ARE SHOWN BESIDE A BULLBOAT.

MEDICINE WHEELS

THE BIGHORN MEDICINE WHEEL IN WYOMING IS LAID OUT WITH STONES ACROSS A LARGE AREA. THE FENCE PROTECTING IT IS HUNG WITH CEREMONIAL OFFERINGS.

Plains peoples of the contact period and today recognize the circle as a sacred and powerful symbol representing the continuing cycle of life and the unity of all natural things. When a cross is placed inside the circle, the symbol is known as a "medicine wheel."

In many areas of the Great Plains, archaeologists have found circles on the ground made by placing individual rocks close to one another in the form of a ring. At some sites, evidence shows that the stones were used to hold down the ends of tipi covers. When the people moved camp, they simply left the stones in place.

These circles are called "tipi rings" and are not very wide in diameter.

But other circles have been found that could not have been used as tipi rings, for they were formed in areas that would have been poor campsites, lacking water and sheltering trees. These circles are distinct in that they often have straight lines of rocks within them, forming what look like the spokes of a wheel. These, too, are known as medicine wheels. Although no one really knows how these rings were used, some archaeologists think that they were built as a kind of calendar to help keep track of the change of seasons. Others believe they may have been used for ceremonies. Because the medicine wheel is still a sacred symbol to the Plains peoples, archaeologists assume that it had the same importance to the ancient peoples of the region.

One of the most well known and impressive of these circles is Bighorn Medicine Wheel in Wyoming. Bighorn Medicine Wheel has a diameter of seventy-five feet (23m), with twenty-eight spokes (lines of rocks) and a pile of rocks at the center that forms the hub of the wheel.

The Spiritual Life

The Plains peoples' belief in the spirit world was an important part of everyday life. For the Plains peoples, everything in the natural world was alive with a vibrant force that was part of the Creator. Because all natural things shared this bond, it was believed that all creatures were related. Thus, a person was expected to show respect not only toward fellow human beings, but also toward all living things.

Almost all activities involved giving thanks to or asking for help from the spirit world. When someone was sick, for example, a medicine man or woman, often using herbs and natural medicines, performed rituals in which the spirits were called to help heal the patient. Before setting out on a hunt, rituals were held that addressed the spirits in the hope of enlisting their aid. Men going to war often carried small leather pouches, called "medicine bundles" or "medicine pouches," that contained objects (usually made of bone, feather, stone, antler, or fur) infused with supernatural power to protect them.

Larger medicine bundles containing powerful objects wrapped in whole animal skins or large

A Plains man sits alone on a vision quest in this painting by Frederic Remington.

pouches were kept by a few members of the group and were opened only during special rituals and ceremonies. Some of these bundles also contained sacred pipes used to smoke tobacco. Acting as a link between human beings and the supernatural forces, the sacred pipe was smoked as an act of prayer. Among the Blackfeet, for example, a ceremony was held each spring in which the sacred Thunder Pipe was taken out of its medicine bundle and smoked when the first thunder of the season was heard. The Thunder Pipe was said to be a gift from Thunder to the Blackfeet people. Using it in a ceremony protected the people from the dangers of lightning, sickness, and enemies. It also offered general protection and well-being for the entire tribe.

While some Plains rituals and ceremonies involved the entire community, others were more personal. The vision quest, for example, was a highly personal ritual undertaken by an individual under the supervision of a medicine person. During the vision quest, a person went alone into the wilderness for four days, praying and fasting in the hope of being granted a message from the spirits in the form of a vision. Both boys and girls could go on vision quests, although girls did not go on them as often. An individual went on a vision quest for the first time during adolescence and continued to go on vision quests throughout life to gain spiritual strength and seek guidance from the spirits.

PLACING THE COVER ON A SWEAT LODGE.

Before the vision quest or any other ritual or ceremony was held, participants purified themselves in a sweat lodge, a dome-shaped structure of saplings and bison hides. During this purification ritual, participants prayed within the lodge while pouring water over heated rocks. This caused the sweat lodge to fill with a hot steam that cleansed and purified the participants.

For many of the Plains peoples, the largest and most sacred ceremony was the Sun Dance, held each year during the summer months. This ceremony usually lasted twelve days, four of which involved fasting, dancing, and piercing of the flesh as the participants prayed continually. It was a time for members of the community to give thanks to the Creator, to ask for help, and to become closer to the spirit world by denying themselves the usual comforts of the body. The Sun Dance was believed to cause good things to happen and to strengthen the tribe as well as the individual participants.

CONCLUSION

Modern Plains Life

Contact with Europeans and their goods brought many changes for the Plains peoples. In addition to horses, guns, beads, knives, and other trade items, European contact also brought new diseases, including smallpox, which killed thousands of Native Americans of the Plains and millions throughout the Western Hemisphere. The presence of Europeans also meant facing new challenges as the newcomers moved westward and made changes to the land. One of the most significant changes was the mass slaughter of the bison herds.

The bison, the most important animal to the Plains peoples, nearly became extinct in the 1800s because the herds were being overhunted by non-Native Americans. Passengers on the newly built transcontinental railroad often shot bison from the trains for sport. Sometimes the herds would cross the tracks and cause long delays. Because of this inconvenience, large numbers of animals were killed. Bison were also killed for profit; their shaggy hides were sold for robes, and their tongues were sold as a delicacy to be eaten.

Hostilities began to heat up between the Plains peoples and the newcomers crossing their region. Signed agreements, called "treaties," between the Plains nations and the United States government were made beginning in the mid-1800s, but so many were broken by the government that the Plains nations became frustrated.

Eventually, wars erupted between the Plains peoples and the United States government. By the late 1800s, the Plains peoples had been confined to reservations, specific areas of land designated by the government and overseen by government agents. Here the Plains peoples were taught a new faith, Christianity, while their traditional religious practices were suppressed. With the bison nearly gone and a new religion pressed upon them, the lifestyle of the Plains peoples was greatly changed.

Confinement on reservations during the nineteenth century resulted in a changed way of life that in many ways brought misery to the Plains peoples. Stripped of their independent lifestyles, their customs and spiritual traditions greatly suppressed, the Plains peoples had to rely on the government for all their needs. But these needs were not always met. Although the government was responsible for providing food and other supplies, the Plains peoples did not always get what they needed due to unreliable transportation and corrupt agents. As a result of this and other factors, conditions on many of the reservations were extremely harsh: poverty, sickness, and near-starvation were widespread.

During this time of great distress, a new, inspirational religion arose called the "Ghost Dance religion." The Ghost Dance religion was started by a prophet of the Paiute nation named Wovoka. (The Paiute live in the Great Basin west of the Plains.) Wovoka claimed to have had a vision in which he was told how to lead the people in this new religious movement. According to his vision, if people performed a dance ceremony wearing certain symbols on their clothing, the old ways of the Plains peoples would return: non-Indians would leave, the bison would return, and relatives who had died would come back alive. Perhaps the most important part of the ceremony was when the dancers fell into trances. During the trances, it was believed, the dancers spoke with the spirits of deceased relatives. Faced with a bleak future, the Plains peoples quickly adopted this new religion, which spread throughout the region.

🌾 WOVOKA, ALSO KNOWN AS JACK WILSON, WAS THE FOUNDER OF THE GHOST DANCE RELIGION.

🌾 A young dancer in full regalia attends a
Native American festival called a "powwow."

However, the Ghost Dance religion did not remain
widespread for long. It quickly declined after an event
that occurred in the winter of 1890 at Wounded Knee,
South Dakota. There, a group of about 350 Lakota, most
of them women and children, were camped under the
watch of the cavalry, which numbered about five hundred men. (The cavalry had been searching for the
group, which was traveling to a place called Pine Ridge.

The group had been ordered to remain in a certain
area of the reservation, and the cavalry had been
ordered to bring them back.) While camped at
Wounded Knee, the Lakota were involved in a Ghost
Dance when the soldiers were ordered to disarm the
men. During the disarming, a shot was fired. (There is
still a great deal of confusion as to whether the shot
was fired accidently or not, and who fired it.) When
this happened, everyone panicked: more shots were
fired and the cavalry began using cannons; by the
time the ordeal was over, about 150 Lakota and about
thirty soldiers had been killed. Today, in the village of

Wounded Knee on the Pine Ridge Reservation, a memorial stands for the Lakota who died there.

Today, many Plains peoples continue to live on the reservations established by the government in the last century. But many also leave the reservations, which offer only limited employment, to find work elsewhere. Some leave to attend college, while some remain and attend tribal colleges on some of the reservations. At the tribal colleges, students learn not only subjects such as business, chemistry, and accounting, but traditional Native languages, culture, and philosophy as well.

Many traditional aspects of Plains culture are still valued by Plains peoples today, including the importance of family ties, generosity, and faith in traditional spirituality. Although many Plains peoples are now Christians, many also take part in traditional rituals and ceremonies. Once outlawed, Plains spiritual practices have resurfaced in the past few decades. Arts such as quillwork and beadwork are still taught and practiced, stories are still told, and Plains languages are still spoken and taught to the younger generation. The peoples of the Plains continue to draw strength from their traditions.

🌿 YOUNG PEOPLE ON THE PINE RIDGE RESERVATION VISIT THE MEMORIAL WHERE THE LAKOTA WHO DIED AT WOUNDED KNEE IN 1890 ARE BURIED.

PLACES TO VISIT

🌿

A trip to the Great Plains offers a variety of interesting places for visitors to learn about the peoples of the Plains. Listed here are only a few:

Akta Lakota Museum
Chamberlain, South Dakota

Bear Butte State Park
Sturgis, South Dakota

The Glenbow Museum
Calgary, Alberta, Canada

Little Bighorn Battlefield National Monument
Crow Agency, Montana

Museum of the Plains Indian
Browning, Montana

Pawnee Indian Village Museum
Republic, Kansas

Pipestone National Monument
Pipestone, Minnesota

Plains Indian Museum
Cody, Wyoming

Provincial Museum of Alberta
Edmonton, Alberta, Canada

Southern Plains Indian Museum
Anadarko, Oklahoma

🌿 World Time Line

8000 B.C.	Pleistocene ends around the world.

5000–250 B.C.

Plains:
Archaic period.

The World:
Neolithic occurs in Europe (about 4000 to 2400 B.C.); Sumerians develop cuneiform writing (about 3000 B.C.); King Tutankhamen is buried in Egypt (about 1323 B.C.); Phoenicians dominate trade in the Mediterranean (about 1200 to 300 B.C.).

250 B.C.–A.D. 950

Plains:
Plains Woodland period (began about 500 B.C.).

The World:
Oldest known text of the Dead Sea scrolls are written (between about 100 B.C. and A.D. 100); The Roman emperor Constantine the Great dies (A.D. 337); Islamic Empire at its peak (about A.D. 850).

A.D. 950–1550
(European contact)

Plains:
Plains Village period.

The World:
The Black Death strikes Europe (mid-1300s); Aztecs found their capital city, Tenochtitlán (about 1325).

A.D. 1550–1700

Plains:
A few of the Plains groups make contact with European explorers and traders.

The World:
Queen Elizabeth rules England (1558–1603); the Mogul Empire flourishes in India; the kingdom of Benin flourishes in West Africa.

A.D. 1700–1900

Plains:
Horses are widespread on the Great Plains. Traditional nomadic cultures of the western plains flourish.

The World:
Captain Cook explores the Southern Hemisphere (1768–1779); the Mexican War is fought between the United States and Mexico (1846–1848); the Industrial Revolution is under way in Western Europe.

✦ Glossary

Archaic — The period following the Pleistocene. On the Great Plains, the Archaic occurred between about 5000 and 250 B.C.

awl — A pointed tool used to punch holes in hides so that the hides may be sewn together.

calumet — A hollow reed with a fan of eagle feathers attached to it, used to perform adoptions and to form alliances between groups.

counting coup — The traditional way of Plains combat, in which a warrior brought honor to himself and his people by doing any number of courageous acts.

High Plains — The drier, western plains, also known as the Short Grass Plains, where grasses range in height from less than two feet to about four feet (60 to 122cm) tall.

medicine bundle — A leather pouch or whole animal skin that contained objects infused with supernatural power.

medicine wheel — A symbol in the form of a circle with a cross in the middle, representing the cycle of life and the unity of all natural things.

Mummy Cave — A site in Wyoming where archaeologists have uncovered artifacts made by early Plains peoples spanning a period of more than five thousand years.

nomadic — Moving from place to place, usually in search of a food supply and other natural resources, such as water.

Olsen-Chubbuck — The site of an early bison hunt in Colorado where archaeologists have uncovered the remains of nearly two hundred bison.

oral tradition — A system whereby information is passed from generation to generation orally (by remembering and retelling stories).

Glossary (Continued)

Paleo-Indians   Refers to Native Americans living during the Pleistocene.

parfleche   A rectangular container made of rawhide and used to store pemmican.

pemmican   A food made of dried meat, dried chokecherries, and boiled fat.

petroglyph   A figure or design carved into rock.

pictograph   A picture that represents an event or an idea.

Pleistocene   A period of earth's history, during which the earth was experiencing several Ice Ages, ending about 8000 B.C.

Prairie   The eastern part of the Great Plains, where there is twenty to fourty inches (50 to 100cm) of rainfall per year and the grasses generally grow at least five feet (1½m) high.

projectile point   Stone point attached to a shaft to make an arrow or a spear.

sedentary   Living in one place throughout the year.

Sun Dance   The most sacred of Plains ceremonies, involving praying, dancing, fasting, and piercing of the flesh.

travois   An A-shaped device, used to drag loads when traveling.

vision quest   A ritual during which an individual went alone into the wilderness to pray and fast in the hope of being granted a message from the spirits.

winter count   A type of record or calendar made by painting pictographs on a hide, each pictograph representing a single year.

🌿 Bibliography

Bancroft-Hunt, Norman. *The Indians of the Great Plains*. New York: William Morrow and Company, 1982.

Holder, Preston. *The Hoe and the Horse on the Plains*. Lincoln, Nebr.: University of Nebraska Press, 1970.

Josephy, Alvin M., Jr. *The Indian Heritage of America*. New York: Alfred A. Knopf, 1985.

Kopper, Philip. *The Smithsonian Book of North Amer-ican Indians: Before the Coming of the Europeans*. Washington, D.C.: Smithsonian Books, 1986.

Lowie, Robert H. *Indians of the Plains*. Garden City, N.Y.: The Natural History Press, 1963.

Snow, Dean. *The Archaeology of North America*. New York: The Viking Press, 1976.

Thomas, David Hurst. *Exploring Ancient Native America: An Archaeological Guide*. New York: Macmillan, 1994.

Photography Credits

Index